FLAGS OF
TENNESSEE

FLAGS
OF
TENNESSEE

By Devereaux D. Cannon, Jr.
Illustrated by Debra Lee Tullier

PELICAN PUBLISHING COMPANY
GRETNA 1990

Library of Congress Cataloging-in-Publication Data

Cannon, Devereaux D., 1954–
    Flags of Tennessee / by Devereaux D. Cannon, Jr. ; illustrated by
Debra Lee Tullier
      p. cm.
    Summary: An illustrated history of the flags that have flown over
the state of Tennessee. Includes foreign, Indian, Civil War, county,
and city flags.
    ISBN 0-88289-794-2
    1. Flags—Tennessee—Juvenile literature. 2. Tennessee—
History—Juvenile literature. [1. Flags—Tennessee—History.
2. Tennessee—History.] I. Tullier, Debra Lee, ill. II. Title.
CR114.T2C36   1990
929.9′2′09768—dc20
                                       90-7679
                                         CIP
                                         AC

Manufactured in Hong Kong

Published by Pelican Publishing Company, Inc.
1101 Monroe Street, Gretna, Louisiana 70053

Contents

FLAGS OF TENNESSEE

Acknowledgments

Special thanks are due to the following people for their assistance in the preparation of this book:

Dr. Whitney Smith, Director, Flag Research Center, Winchester, Massachusetts

Dan Agent, Cherokee Nation Communications, Cherokee Nation, Tahlequah, Oklahoma

Emil Farve, Chickasaw Nation, Ada, Oklahoma

Hon. Truman Clark, County Executive, and Joanie Smith, Secretary, Carter County, Tennessee

Harry Banniza, Assistant Director of the Department of General Services, Metropolitan Government of Nashville and Davidson County, Tennessee

Hon. Dalton Roberts, County Executive of Hamilton County, Tennessee

Hon. James R. Patterson, County Executive, Hardin County, Tennessee

Joe M. Hamby, Director of Purchasing and Personnel, Knox County, Tennessee

Hon. Mike Greene, County Executive, Maury County, Tennessee

Hon. William N. Morris, Jr., Mayor, Shelby County, Tennessee

Keith Westmoreland, County Executive, and Joe Mike Akard, Purchasing Agent, Sullivan County, Tennessee

Scott Shelton, Administrative Assistant, city of Clarksville, Tennessee

Hon. Bobby Jones, Mayor, and Nancy W. Allen, Administrative Assistant, city of Goodlettsville, Tennessee

Hon. Charles H. Farmer, Mayor of Jackson, Tennessee

FLAGS OF TENNESSEE

Kippy Benedict, Manchester Area Chamber of Commerce, Manchester, Tennessee

Dorothy Osradker, Assistant City Attorney, city of Memphis, Tennessee

Evonne J. Phifer, Finance Director, city of Paris, Tennessee

Introduction

Every nation of the earth, every state of the American union, every ship at sea, and every Boy Scout troop have one thing in common: flags. No political event, parade, or carnival is complete without flags. Their colors and the sound of their snap in the wind add a note of gaiety to the most solemn event.

Flags have been used by the human race for over five thousand years. Basically a form of signpost to identify some person, place, or entity, the emblems of heraldic art worked into cloth often assume for us an identity of their own. The sense of cultural identity which can attach itself to flags can assume almost idolatrous proportions. The outrage felt by a war veteran when his country's flag is defiled is similar to that felt by a Christian at the desecration of a crucifix.

Because of the fascination that flags hold for us, they can prove to be a useful tool in the teaching of history. History is the study of the movement of man and his governments through time and space, and that movement has been attended by the banners representative of those governments. The people of former colonial possessions, especially the states and nations of the Americas and Africa, have a colorful history from a vexillologist's (flag historian's) perspective because they have been the object of the imperialistic designs of so many other nations, and have often changed hands a number of times before assuming a self-governing status.

The history of Tennessee is illustrative of that general rule. While Tennessee is about to celebrate the bicentenary of its admission to the union of American states, the history of the colonial exploitation of that land by Europe extended back in time another two hundred years and more. During that time the native population enjoyed the commerce with, and lost its land to, the representatives of three European powers. In the pages which follow, we will take a look at the history of those times and learn of the European flags which once claimed dominion over the land now know as Tennessee.

9

FLAGS OF TENNESSEE

We will then move to the time of revolution, when the English colonists would throw off the chains of colonial rule and "assume among the powers of the earth, the separate and equal station to which the laws of nature and of nature's God" entitled them. This event opened a whole new era of flags, when Tennesseans would follow banners representative of self-government, rather than allegiance to distant kings.

Let us proceed, then, and take a look at the flags which have been associated with the history of Tennessee.

FLAGS OF
TENNESSEE

PART I

FLAGS OF THE STATE

CHAPTER 1
A Brief Look at Tennessee Geography

Travellers to Tennessee were once greeted at her borders by signs welcoming them to "the Three States of Tennessee." Politically, culturally, and geologically, Tennessee is indeed three separate regions. The state is officially divided into three Grand Divisions, which are represented by the three stars on the Tennessee flag. Each "Division" is identified by a different geology and topography, which resulted in distinct cultural development.

East Tennessee is composed of the Unaka and Great Smoky Mountains and the eastern valley of the Tennessee River, and is separated from Middle Tennessee by the Cumberland Plateau. The whole region is rich in minerals and East Tennessee is among the leading producers of marble in America. The mountainous terrain makes East Tennessee the state's least productive area in agriculture, although farming flourishes in the rich Tennessee valley. The Cumberland Plateau, which divides East and Middle Tennessee, contains the majority of the state's coal deposits.

Middle Tennessee, west of the plateau, is divided geologically into the Highland Rim and the Central Basin. The hills of the Highland Rim are good farmland. The Central Basin of the Cumberland River, however, is recognized as the most productive land

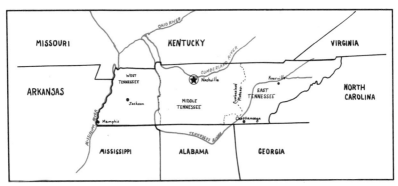

A map of Tennessee showing the Grand Divisions and the main geological features

15

in the state's agricultural industry. It is devoted largely to pasture and is similar to the Blue Grass region of Kentucky.

West Tennessee extends from the western valley of the Tennessee River to the Mississippi valley. With nary a hill in sight, the rich alluvial soil of this Grand Division accounts for the bulk of Tennessee's cotton and soybean production.

CHAPTER 2
The Tennessee Flag

On April 17, 1905, the Tennessee General Assembly adopted a flag for the state of Tennessee. The Volunteer State had previously adopted a state flag, but its design was not popular, and the flag was not often used. A Johnson City lawyer and soldier decided that Tennessee could do better.

Captain Le Roy Reeves, commander of Company F, 3rd Tennessee Infantry, designed a flag having a blue disc bearing three white stars centered on a field of crimson. The blue was separated from the red by a narrow white edging, and a white strip also formed the border between the crimson field and a vertical blue bar on the fly edge (see glossary) of the flag. Captain Reeves's flag bill was sponsored in the General Assembly by Representative Walter W. Faw and Senator Douglas Wilkie. The bill was enacted as Chapter 498 of the *Public Acts of 1905*, and is now codified as *Tennessee Code Annotated* section 4–1–301. The flag was first flown

The flag of Tennessee

over the East Tennessee State Normal School (now East Tennessee State University) in Reeves's hometown of Johnson City.

Captain Reeves explained the design of his flag as follows:

> The three stars are of pure white, representing the three grand divisions of the State. They are bound together by the endless circle of the blue field, the symbol being three bound together in one—an indissoluble trinity. The large field is crimson. The final blue bar relieves the sameness of the crimson field and prevents the flag from showing too much crimson when hanging limp. The white edgings contrast more strongly the other colors.

Those familiar with Tennessee's geography and politics have no trouble identifying the meaning of the three stars. Culturally and geologically, East, Middle, and West Tennessee are as different as any three states could be. Yet non-Tennesseans are often confused about the symbolism of the tri-star flag.

In its October 1917 issue, *National Geographic* magazine featured a colorful and detailed article about the flags of the world. The author of the article was apparently not familiar with Tennessee, and, rather than consulting Tennessee sources for an explanation of her flag, he seems to have invented a theory based upon the coincidence that Tennessee was the sixteenth state to be admitted to the American Union, i.e., the third after the original thirteen.

The *National Geographic* article was so widely circulated, and the prestige of that journal so great, that this erroneous notion of Tennessee's three stars became widely accepted. As a result, in 1920 John Trotwood Moore, director of the Tennessee Department of Library, Archives and History (now the State Library and Archives), asked the flag's designer to explain the meaning of the stars. After reasserting that the stars represented the Grand Divisions of the state, Captain Reeves went on to say:

> I remember to have seen published in the past a statement that the three stars were intended to represent the fact that Tennessee, which was the sixteenth state to be admitted, was the third state after the original thirteen. I had nothing of the kind in mind when I designed the flag prior to its adoption in 1905.

Ever since, every publication by the state of Tennessee on the design and meaning of the Tennessee flag has emphasized that the stars represent the Grand Divisions of the state. Yet the misinformation published by the *National Geographic* in 1917 continues to be republished by sources outside of Tennessee.

The Tennessee Flag

Another common problem with the Tennessee flag is the issue of "which way is up." Despite the generally good example of the state government, as often as not Tennesseans will fly their flag upside down. The United States Postal Service helped to compound the problem in 1976, when a series of postage stamps was issued featuring the flags of the states. The Tennessee flag stamp displayed the flag upside down. Despite protests by state officials, the Postal Service insisted that the stamp was correct, and continued to print Tennessee's flag belly-up.

The Tennessee flag law specifies:

> The arrangement of the three (3) stars shall be such that the centers of no two stars shall be in a line parallel to either the side or the end of the flag, but intermediate between the same; and the highest star shall be the one nearest the upper confined corner of the flag.

The law also specifies that the circular blue field, not including the white margin, is to have a diameter equal to one-half the width of the flag. Flag manufacturers often ignore that specification, and at times flags can be seen on which the blue disc occupies almost all of the red field.

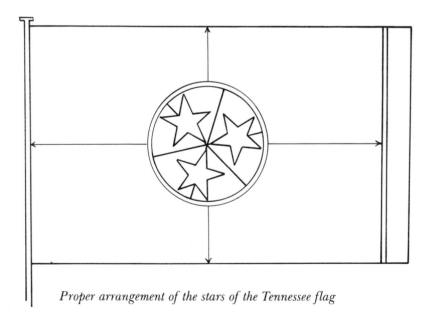

Proper arrangement of the stars of the Tennessee flag

CHAPTER 3
Flags of the Governor and the General Assembly

FLAG OF THE GOVERNOR

No law of Tennessee authorizes a flag for the governor of the state. In 1939, however, the adjutant general of Tennessee requested the United States Department of War to design a flag for Tennessee's chief executive.

Flag of the governor

The flag produced by the War Department features a green hickory tree (reminiscent of Andrew Jackson, "Old Hickory") centered on a red field. The tree stands upon a heraldic wreath of white and red, and on the tree are found the three stars of Tennessee, arranged to fit the shape of the foliage. Finally, the flag is adorned with four white stars, one in each corner of the red field, indicating the Governor's constitutional rank as commander-in-chief of the military forces of Tennessee.

21

FLAG OF THE GENERAL ASSEMBLY

In the late 1970s a competition was initiated among Tennessee students to design a flag for the state legislature. The winning entry, by Sheila Adkins of Fulton High School in Knoxville, was adopted by the General Assembly in 1978.

Flag of the Tennessee General Assembly

The flag is a field of white, bordered above and below by equal stripes of red, white and blue, the blue being the outermost stripe on top and bottom. Three large red stars, again representing the three Grand Divisions, are arranged in a horizontal line across the center of the white field. Slanted across the center star is a golden gavel, representing the power of the people vested in the legislature. The center star is also encircled by a golden wreath of wheat, around which, in black, are the words "General Assembly of Tennessee."

CHAPTER 4
Past State Flags

Prior to 1861, no effort was made to adopt a flag for the state of Tennessee. A common tradition among state militias of the nineteenth century was to carry as the state colors a blue flag decorated with the state seal, and such a flag may have been used by Tennessee troops; but otherwise, the state government was happy to operate solely under the flag of the United States.

This comfortable state of affairs came to an abrupt end in 1861. With the election of Abraham Lincoln to the presidency on the ticket of a sectional party and with only about 40 percent of the popular vote, the people of South Carolina decided that the American Union could no longer insure domestic tranquility, and therefor chose, as they had done in the Declaration of Independence in 1776, "to assume, among the powers of the earth, the separate and equal station to which the laws of nature and of nature's God entitle them." South Carolina was followed by other states of the deep South which, on February 8, 1861, joined together to form a new federal government called the Confederate States of America.

Tennessee did not immediately join the movement for Southern independence. Although the state government was inclined toward secession, the people as a whole were more patient and on February 9, 1861 voted by a three to one margin against leaving the Union. After Lincoln's government attempted to reinforce Fort Sumter, however, resulting in the bombardment and surrender of the fort, it became clear to Tennesseans that Lincoln was determined to wage war to conquer the seceded states. When faced with the choice of fighting with the North for conquest or with the South for self-government, the Volunteer State chose the South.

PROPOSED FLAG OF 1861

When the legislature met in a special session after Lincoln's call for troops to invade the Confederate States, the clear purpose was to cast Tennessee's lot with the South. Customarily a flag was flown over the capitol when the legislature was in session, but it seemed inappropriate under the circumstances to fly the flag of the United

23

States. Nor was it deemed proper to fly the Confederate flag, since Tennessee had not yet seceded.

On April 25, 1861, the first day of the special legislative session, Senate Speaker Tazewell B. Newman introduced a resolution for the adoption of a state flag. The design proposed by Senator Newman was the flag adopted by the Confederate States, with the coat of arms of Tennessee on the same.

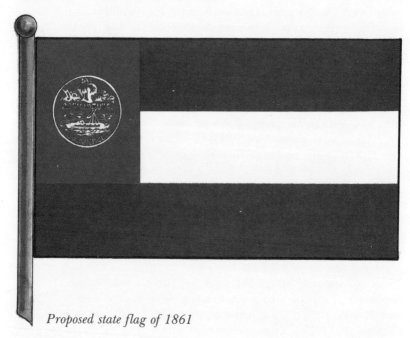

Proposed state flag of 1861

The flag was not adopted, the legislature apparently believing it inappropriate to adopt what was so obviously a secession flag before secession was accomplished; but several Tennessee regiments in the Confederate army carried flags which were very similar to Senator Newman's design. Tennessee would not adopt a state flag in 1861, but left the capitol's pole bare until the flag of the Confederate States was raised for the first time on the evening of Monday, June 17, 1861.

FLAG OF THE 1880s

After the war the Tennessee legislature still took no action to adopt a state flag, but the Military Department of the state government apparently did so on its own. On June 13, 1886, in answer to an inquiry made by Messrs. Baird & Dillon of New York City regarding the state flag, General R. W. Cantrell, adjutant general of the Tennessee Militia, wrote that

> the Tennessee State Flag is of heavy double blue silk[,] 6 by 6 1/2 feet[,] gold cord and tassels & heavy gold fringe & with the Coat of Arms of [the] State on either side—circled with oak wreath. Staff 10 feet & mounted with Gold Eagle.

The flag described by General Cantrell in 1886 is essentially the same as the militia flags used prior to 1861.

Tennessee flag in 1880s

THE FLAG OF 1897

The first day of June 1896 marked the 100th anniversary of the admission of Tennessee as a member state of the American Union. The state authorities, however, were late in properly celebrating the event and, although a token opening of the centennial celebration was made on that date, it was not until almost a year later that the great Centennial Exposition in Nashville began.

In keeping with the tardiness regarding the centennial festivities, the legislature seemed to have finally recognized the fact that Tennessee had no official flag. On April 30, 1897, the day before the opening of the Centennial Exposition, the General Assembly adopted a resolution which began, "Whereas, the State of Tennessee has no official flag," and went on to remedy that lack.

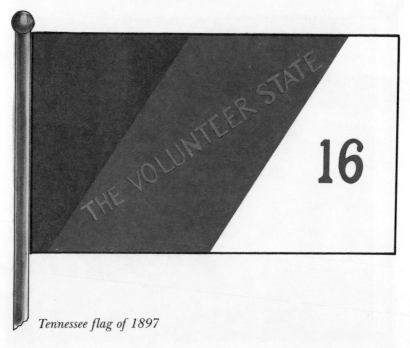

Tennessee flag of 1897

The new flag was a diagonal tricolor of red, blue and white, so shaped in order to represent the geographical lines of the three Grand Divisions of the state. The white section at the fly end of the flag displayed the blue numeral "16," representing Tennessee's numerical position among the states of the Union, while the nickname

"THE VOLUNTEER STATE" was placed diagonally across the blue bar of the flag in yellow or gold letters.

Flags of this design, or something like them, were used at the Centennial Exposition, though not all necessarily adhered to the letter of the law. One such example on display at the Tennessee State Museum exchanged the positions of the colored panels, and moved the "16," now in white on blue, to the hoist (see glossary) rather than the fly end of the flag.

Although the flag continued to be used in some ceremonial functions after 1897, it was not popular, and its very existence was unknown even to some of the most capable Tennessee historians.

PART II

HISTORIC FLAGS OF TENNESSEE

CHAPTER 5
The Aboriginal Nations of Tennessee

In the sixteenth century, when Europeans first made contact with the land that was to become Tennessee, the two nations which held dominion over most of that territory were the Cherokee and the Chickasaw. The Cherokee were dominant in the east and the Chickasaw in the west. Middle Tennessee was essentially uninhabited at that time. All of the country bounded on the north by the Ohio River, on the east by the Cumberland Plateau, and on the south and west by the Tennessee River was a vast hunting ground claimed by the Cherokee, Creek, Chickasaw, and Shawnee Nations. Wars brought on by these conflicting claims depopulated the area, and gave that portion north of the Cumberland River the name "Dark and Bloody Ground."

With a population in the neighborhood of twenty thousand, the Cherokee were the largest nation in the American South. Their people resided in sixty towns mainly located in East Tennessee, western North Carolina, and northern Georgia, and they claimed an empire that took in, additionally, Middle Tennessee, most of Kentucky, and parts of Alabama, South Carolina, and Virginia.

The Cherokee Nation was actually a confederation of seven clans, and the Cherokee's primary loyalty was to his clan. Cherokee society was founded upon a matriarchal base, with lineage and clan membership determined through the line of one's mother.

Cherokee society was stratified in the roles allotted. Agriculture was "women's work," in which men did not participate, while hunting was the sole domain of the males. Furthermore, the clans were divided between "white" and "red" clans, with the former having responsibility for peaceful pursuits, and the latter, the art of war.

The Cherokee did not shrink from war, and some reports indicate that military pursuits were a passion for the nation. At one time, when entreated to end a war with the Tuscaroras, the Cherokee response is said to have been, "We cannot live without war. Should we make peace with the Tuscaroras . . . we must immediately look for some other, with whom we can engage in our beloved occupation."

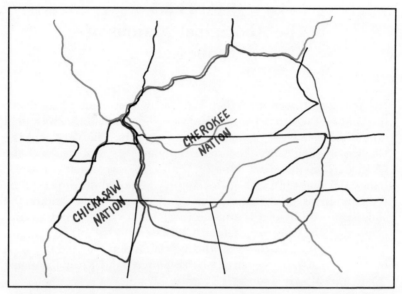

Map showing the claims of the Cherokee and Chickasaw Nations

The Chickasaw Nation claimed a large portion of northern Mississippi as well as all of Tennessee and Kentucky west of the Tennessee River. Most of their towns were situated along the Mississippi River, with the vast territory of their claims in West Tennessee reserved as hunting lands.

The Chickasaw were ruled by an elected chief or king whose title was *mingo*, and who was chosen from the *Koi*, or "peaceful," division of the nation. A war chief would be chosen from the *Ishpani*, or "military" division. The *mingo*, however, took precedence over the war chief when he accompanied a military operation. Like the Cherokee, the Chickasaw figured their descent through the maternal line. The Chickasaw also tended to divide work duties along sexual lines, but not so strictly as the Cherokee.

Unlike the Cherokee, the Chickasaw were not eager or anxious for war. When they determined to fight, it was after due and cool deliberation. Yet in war, the Chickasaw were as fierce an opponent as any, and often prevailed over more "warlike" nations.

The Chickasaw had joined with the Cherokee to expel the Shawnee from Middle Tennessee, and the two nations had been allies on other occasions. Yet in 1769 the Cherokee Nation went to war with their less aggressive neighbors, only to suffer a crushing defeat at just the time that Englishmen first sought to settle Cherokee lands in the Watauga district of East Tennessee.

CHEROKEE AND CHICKASAW FLAGS

The Native American nations did not use "national" flags as we think of them. However, after coming into contact with white civilization, the Cherokee determined to try to avoid extinction by adapting to white culture. This did not prove an altogether successful experiment, as is attested to by the infamous "Trail of Tears," which saw most of the nation forced to move to Oklahoma, leaving only a remnant in hiding in the mountains of Tennessee and North Carolina. Yet they did adapt, in many ways becoming more "civilized" than their white invaders.

The oldest known Cherokee flag is one carried by Cherokee soldiers of the Confederate army in their new lands west of Arkansas (modern Oklahoma). This flag was the Confederate "Stars and Bars," with the circle of white stars, representing the states of the Confederacy, surrounding five red stars, which represented the five Indian nations in alliance with the Confederacy.

The flag of the Cherokee Nation

The present flag of the Cherokee Nation displays the national seal in black and gold on an orange field. Seven stars are arrayed around the seal, representing the seven clans of the Cherokee Nation. In the upper fly corner is a single black star to commemorate the approximately five thousand Cherokees who perished on the "Trail of Tears." The entire flag is edged with a black and green "rope" border.

The flag of the Chickasaw Nation

Like the Cherokee, the Chickasaw Nation is currently located in Oklahoma. Their flag follows the tradition of a number of American states in placing the national seal on a dark blue field. The seal, which was authorized by the Chickasaw Constitution adopted in 1856, depicts a Chickasaw warrior holding in his right hand two arrows, representing the *Koi* and *Ishpani* divisions of the nation. His left hand grasps a bow, and a war shield is slung on his left arm.

CHAPTER 6
The Spanish Claims

By virtue of the discoveries of Columbus, the Kingdom of Spain laid claim to an empire that contained all of North America, including our Tennessee. Discovery alone would not suffice, however, to retain such an empire, and the armies of Spain set about the task of conquering and exploiting their king's new domains. Mexico, Central America, and Peru quickly fell to the Conquistadores, but the more northern lands would prove a harder nut to crack.

In 1521 Ponce de León, the discoverer of Florida, was killed and his settlement destroyed. In 1524 a Spanish army commanded by Lucas Vasquez de Ayllon was destroyed by Indians in either Georgia or South Carolina. In 1528 another attempt to take Florida for Spain was made by Pamphilo de Narvaez. Sailing from Cuba with over 400 men, Narvaez met with disaster at sea and Indians who violently resisted invasion. Narvaez died and only five of his party returned.

Against this background, eleven years after the destruction of the Narvaez group, Hernando De Soto set out with an expedition designed to open the vast territory north of Florida to Spanish exploitation. De Soto was no novice to exploration. He had campaigned in Central America, and been Pizarro's lieutenant in the conquest of Peru. Leaving Cuba with an army of 620 men, De Soto set out on a trek that would carry him across a large portion of the American South, and bring him into contact, and combat, with most of the Indian nations inhabiting that territory. The later Spanish claims to all of this region were based largely upon De Soto's exploits.

De Soto landed at Tampa Bay in Florida on May 30, 1539. His journey north through Florida and Georgia extended into a region that may have included the Carolinas and the southeastern portion of Tennessee. From there the army turned west, passing through Alabama and into Mississippi. Crossing the lands of the Chickasaw, De Soto entered Tennessee from Mississippi, and came upon the Mississippi River at the Fourth Chickasaw Bluff, the present site of Memphis, two years after leaving Florida. The Spaniards crossed into Arkansas, which territory they explored for another year, possibly ranging as far west as Oklahoma. After De Soto died in June 1542, his followers abandoned the expedition, about 300 survivors reaching Mexico in September.

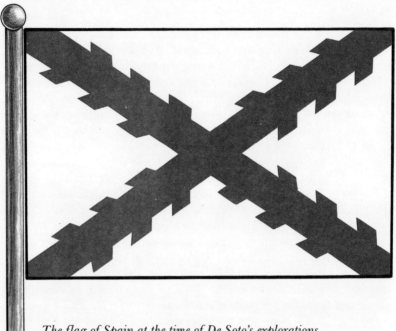

The flag of Spain at the time of De Soto's explorations

King Charles I (also Emperor Charles V of the Holy Roman Empire) assumed the throne of Spain after the death of his grandfather, King Ferdinand, in 1516. Under Ferdinand and Isabella, the flag of Spain had been the quartered (see glossary) arms of Castille and Leon. Charles replaced this with the emblem of his father, the Duke of Burgundy.

The Burgundian flag displayed a red saltire (see glossary), known as the Cross of Saint Andrew, on a white field. It was somewhat similar to the current flag of Alabama, though where the cross of Alabama's flag is plain, that of the Burgundian flag of Spain was in the pattern described in heraldry as raguly. It is said to be derived from an image of two tree trunks crossed, their limbs severed short of the trunk.

Over 250 years would pass from the time of De Soto's discovery of the Mississippi River before another representative of the king of Spain would attempt to establish dominion over a part of Tennessee. During that time Spain's hold on North America had been tenuous. In 1762, during one of England's wars against Spain and France, England had taken Cuba from Spain. The peace treaties of the following year rearranged the map of North America. France gave England all of her land east of the Mississippi except New Orleans. New Orleans and all French claims west of the Mississippi were given to Spain. Finally, England returned Cuba to Spain in exchange for Florida.

All would change again in twenty years. In 1783 a treaty formally ended the American Revolution, and England recognized her former colonies as independent states. The British also gave Florida back to Spain in exchange for the Bahamas. Viewing the new United States as weak, the Spanish governor at New Orleans sought to extend Spain's claim to all of the land explored by De Soto. To defend this claim, Spanish forts were built on the east side of the Mississippi River. One was at Natchez, and another, Fort Barancas, was built in 1794 at the present site of Memphis. After a great deal

The flag of Spain at the time Fort Barancas was built

37

of trouble, during which the Spanish first tried to sway the western settlers to leave the Union in favor of Spain, and failing that, encouraged the various Indian nations to wage war against the Americans, a diplomatic settlement finally resulted in the withdrawal of Spanish claims to any part of Tennessee.

In 1785 King Charles III decreed that the Spanish flag should be a combination of three stripes of red, yellow and red. In 1793 a badge composed of the impaled (see glossary) arms of Castile and Leon was added to the flag. The central yellow stripe of the flag was twice as wide as the red. Except for the badge, the Spanish flag that flew over Fort Barancas is the same as that used by Spain today.

CHAPTER 7
The French Claims

The first permanent French settlement in North America was in 1695 at Port Royal in Nova Scotia, followed three years later by the founding of Quebec. Based upon the 1673 explorations of missionary Father Jacques Marquette, the French extended their territorial claims to all of the land south of the Great Lakes and west of the Appalachians, including within their American empire all that is now Tennessee.

In 1682 the French explorer René Robert Cavalier, the Sieur de la Salle, led an expedition from Lake Michigan, down the Illinois and Mississippi rivers to the mouth of the Mississippi near the site of New Orleans. La Salle gave the name of Louisiana to the entire region of the Mississippi Valley, including present-day West Tennessee, thus reinforcing the French claim to the area.

On his return trip up the Mississippi, la Salle built and garrisoned Fort Prudhomme near the present site of Randolph, estab-

A French flag of the 1700s

lishing the first French settlement in Tennessee. Later, the French built Fort Assumption at the site of Memphis, and a fort near French Lick in what would become Nashville.

The French first built at French Lick about 1714. About 1760 a Frenchman named Timothy de Monbruen selected French Lick as the site of a trading station. De Monbruen (whose name has been spelled de Montbruen, de Mumbreun, DeMumbrune, and a Nashville street named in his memory is spelled Demonbruen) remained at French Lick, despite the surrender of the French claim to the Tennessee area to Great Britain in 1763, and later became a leading citizen of the new settlement called Nashborough.

At the time of the French claim to Tennessee there was no one flag which was recognized as the national flag of France. Apparently the most commonly used flags were white fields covered with gold fleurs-de-lis. Some French flags, however, had only three fleurs-de-lis, some were blue with three fleurs-de-lis, and some were blue with a white cross. French military colors tended to display a white cross, with the four quarters displaying the distinctive colors of the regiment to which the flag belonged. The famous French Tricolor did not become the national flag of France until after the French Revolution, over thirty-five years after France lost any claim to dominion over any part of Tennessee.

CHAPTER 8
British Settlement

Despite the earlier efforts of Spanish and French explorers, the history of European development of the Tennessee area actually began with the movement of the English and Scots-Irish settlers from the British colonies in Virginia and North Carolina.

England's first permanent settlement in America was established at Jamestown, Virginia, in 1607. One hundred years later the American seaboard, from Boston in the Massachusetts Bay Colony to Savannah, Georgia, was a thriving offshoot of mother England. After the French surrender in 1763, England's domains also included Canada and all of the land from the Appalachians to the Mississippi. Even before the western territories had come under British sovereignty, hunters and trappers from Virginia and the Carolinas, including such men as Dr. Thomas Walker and Daniel Boone, were exploring that country. Some of these hunting parties,

Flag of Great Britain

known as "long hunters," would stay in the western territories for a year or more before returning to the East with their pelts.

The Indian nations west of the mountains were unhappy about the encroachments of English settlers into their lands. For a time the king and Parliament of England tried to keep their subjects on the east side of the Appalachians by laws, but these proved ineffective. The next step was to try to buy peace by buying Indian lands. In 1768 the British Indian Commissioners signed treaties with the Cherokee Nation, buying most of their lands between the Tennessee and Ohio rivers. The next year would find William Bean living in what is thought to have been the first European's house built in Tennessee, a log cabin on Boone's Creek at what would become the Watauga settlement in present-day Carter County. Bean's son Russell was the first child of European descent known to have been born in Tennessee.

At the time that British settlers began to move into Tennessee, the flag of Great Britain was the Union Flag which had been designed by King James I over 160 years before. Prior to 1606 England and Scotland had had separate kings and separate flags. The flag of England was white with a red cross, called the cross of St. George. The flag of Scotland was blue with a white cross in the

British Red Ensign

42

shape of an "x," known as the cross of St. Andrew. In 1606 King James became the king of both countries, and combined the two flags to make a single flag for the United Kingdoms of Great Britain. This flag was changed in 1801 by adding the red "x"-shaped cross of St. Patrick to represent Ireland, and the flag of Great Britain is still in that form today.

The Union Flag of Britain was not used to identify ships at sea. Instead, British ships flew a flag known as the Red Ensign, which had a red field with the Union Flag in the upper canton, or corner. Because the majority of American cities in the mid-eighteenth century were coastal towns and ports, the Red Ensign was the British flag most commonly seen by American colonists.

CHAPTER 9
Independence

The French and Indian Wars left England with a large debt, and in 1765 the British Parliament sought to pay the debt in part by taxing the American colonists. Before that time the Parliament had not passed any direct taxes on the colonies, or tried to make any local laws for them, leaving such things to the colonial legislatures.

The colonists objected to the taxes, saying that since Americans were not represented in Parliament, Parliament had no right to tax Americans. The government in England and the royal governors in the colonies snubbed the Americans as impudent commoners whose protestations of "no taxation without representation" were rude and unworthy of consideration. The situation deteriorated over the next ten years.

Among the worst of the royal officials in the colonies was Governor Tryon of North Carolina. His government became so oppressive that the people organized resistance forces known as Regulators to oppose the oppression of the royal government. In May

First flag of the United States

1771 Governor Tryon's royalist army defeated the Regulators at the battle of Alamance Creek. Many of those who escaped fled over the mountains into Tennessee.

The defeat at Alamance Creek did not end resistance to arbitrary government. The North Carolina Assembly continued to press the demands of the people against the royal governor. Because the legislature was so unfriendly to his policies, Governor Tryon ordered it to disband in April 1775. The royal legislature adjourned, and its members immediately resolved themselves into an independent legislature, declaring themselves the lawfully elected representatives of the people, and proceeding with what was in effect the first independent government in North America. While they were in session, the battle of Lexington was fought in Massachusetts and the revolutionary war had begun. North Carolina's independence would be declared the next month, anticipating the Declaration of Independence adopted by the Continental Congress by over a year.

When the Revolution began, there was no common revolutionary flag. Rebel armies and provisional governments used a variety of flags featuring such devices as rattlesnakes, pine trees, crescent moons, and stripes. In May 1775 the Continental Congress, made up of delegates appointed by the revolutionary legislatures, appointed George Washington of Virginia as commander of the non-

The first "Stars and Stripes"

existent Continental Army. Washington began the task of creating that army, and on January 1, 1776 it was formally established. In a ceremony to celebrate that event, a seventy-six-foot pole was erected on Prospect Hill in Somerville, near Boston, and on that New Year's Day a flag to be known as the Grand Union Flag was raised. This Grand Union Flag was soon in use throughout the colonies, and with the adoption of the Declaration of Independence, it became the first national flag of the United States of America. This flag was actually the British Red Ensign with white stripes added to its red field to create a field of thirteen red and white stripes, with the British Union Flag in the upper corner. The Grand Union Flag continued as the provisional American flag until the official adoption of the "Stars and Stripes" on June 14, 1777, and actually continued to be used for some time afterwards.

After the Declaration of Independence, the use of a flag displaying the British Union as an emblem of independent American states was an anachronism whose days were numbered. On June 14, 1777, almost a year after declaring independence, the Continental Congress changed the American flag by removing the crosses of England and Scotland, and replacing them on the blue background with stars for the American states. Although popular legend designs the original "Stars and Stripes" with its stars in a circle, historical evidence indicates that stars arranged in rows was the most common pattern used.

When North Carolina became an independent state, her territory included all of what is now Tennessee. While they were not on the "front lines" of the Revolution, the western settlers, who were called "overmountain men," were by no means left out of the fighting. The British enlisted the aid of the Cherokee Nation, which took to the warpath against North Carolina's overmountain settlers. In 1778 North Carolina created a new county to include its western citizens. Named Washington County, it was the first of many areas to be named for George Washington. In 1780 the settlers of this modern-day Tennessee region were to make an important contribution to the war effort.

In that year the British planned a southern offensive, which would begin at Charleston, South Carolina. The governor of South Carolina asked North Carolinians to come to his aid, and among those to answer his plea were 200 overmountain men. These men joined General McDowell's North Carolina forces, and won a battle at Enoree River. Soon, however, the British under Cornwallis had captured almost every important place in Georgia and the Carolinas. McDowell's little army disbanded, and the Tennesseans returned to their homes over the mountains.

The left wing of the British army was commanded by a colonel named Patrick Ferguson. Ferguson sent word to the overmountain men that he intended to invade their lands and destroy their settlements unless they became loyal subjects of the king. John Sevier and Isaac Shelby, leaders of the Tennessee settlers, decided to meet Ferguson rather than let him bring war to them. Joining with other forces from North Carolina and Virginia, an army of 1,500 men under the command of Colonel William Campbell of Virginia crossed over the mountains. On October 7, 1780, the settler army surrounded Ferguson's troops on King's Mountain, on the border between North and South Carolina. By the end of the day Ferguson was dead, the left wing of the British army was destroyed, and Cornwallis was forced to retreat from North Carolina.

There is no information regarding under what flag, if any, the settlers fought at King's Mountain. Nor is there any reliable information establishing a North Carolina state flag for the period. It is known, however, that North Carolina troops at this time carried some versions of the "Stars and Stripes."

One such flag was used by North Carolina troops at the Battle of Guilford Courthouse on March 15, 1781, five months after King's Mountain. This flag had a field composed of thirteen blue and red

North Carolina Militia flag

stripes. The canton was white and displayed thirteen blue eight-pointed stars.

In 1781 the Articles of Confederation were finally ratified by all thirteen states, and the United States began to formally function under their first Constitution. In 1783 a peace treaty was signed in which Great Britain recognized her former colonies as free and independent states. In 1784 North Carolina turned her western lands over to the Continental Congress, and the people of those lands held a convention which organized the state of Franklin. However, before Congress could accept the lands or admit Franklin to the union, North Carolina revoked its gift of the territory and demanded that the people there disband their new state and return their allegiance to North Carolina. For the next four years a civil war of sorts was fought between the supporters of Franklin and those loyal to North Carolina.

In 1788 the state of Franklin disbanded, and a new Constitution was adopted by the United States. In 1790 North Carolina again voted to give her western lands to the federal government, which accepted those lands that same year, and organized them as the "Territory of the United States South of the River Ohio."

CHAPTER 10
Under the "Stars and Stripes"

When the "Territory South of the River Ohio" was established out of the lands given by North Carolina, the states of the U.S. numbered thirteen, and their flag displayed an equal number of stars and stripes. In 1791, however, Vermont became the fourteenth member of the United States, and the next year Virginia granted independence to her western territories, which were admitted to the union as the Commonwealth of Kentucky. The thirteen stars and stripes now flew over fifteen states.

Flag of the United States from 1795 to 1818

In 1795, almost three years after the admission of Kentucky, that flag was changed to reflect the new states. Beginning on the first day of May 1795 the flag of the United States was to be composed of fifteen stars and fifteen stripes. One year and one month later, Tennessee joined the union as the sixteenth state.

The flag law did not change when Tennessee became a state; nor did it change for Ohio, Louisiana, or Indiana as they were admitted to the American federation. Officially the flag was to remain fifteen stars and stripes. It is known that sixteen-star flags existed, and in 1817 the flag flying over the federal capitol in Washington was made with eighteen stars and an equal number of stripes. Not until 1818 was the law changed to standardize the stripes at thirteen, and to add a star for each new state on the Fourth of July after it entered the union. On July 4, 1818, Tennessee's star was officially added to the flag as one of a total of twenty.

Flag of the United States from 1818 to 1819

The Louisiana Purchase in 1803 had added vast new expanses to the lands of the United States, and new states continued to be established in the territories. By 1845 the number of stars had grown to twenty-seven. The next year another star would be added which would prove fateful to Tennessee and all of North America.

The Republic of Texas had gained her independence in 1836, largely with the help of Tennesseans. The Texan Army had been commanded by former Tennessee governor Sam Houston, who was later elected president of the Republic. For almost ten years Texans governed themselves, but during that time they had courted the United States with an eye towards admission to the union. Northern politicians resisted Texan statehood, fearful of strengthening the South's position in the federal Congress, but finally, in December 1845, a treaty was ratified resulting in the addition of the lone star of Texas to the flag of the United States on July 4, 1846.

Flag of the United States from 1846 to 1847

For the ten years of Texas's independence, Texas and Mexico had disputed the location of their common border. Texas claimed as far south as the Rio Grande, while Mexico maintained that she was sovereign as far north as the Nueces River.

When Texas joined the U.S., her Mexican problem became the problem of the United States. In the spring of 1846 President James K. Polk, a Tennessean, ordered American troops into the disputed territory. They were fired upon by Mexican troops whose job was to hold the territory for their country. Thus began the Mexican War, which resulted in the addition of northern Mexico, from the western reaches of Texas to the California coast, to the territories of the United States.

Tennesseans such as David Crockett and former Tennessee governor Sam Houston had been instrumental in securing Texan independence. Tennesseans were also to be an important part of winning the war brought on by the admission of Texas to the United

States. Governor Aaron V. Brown called for 2,600 Tennesseans to volunteer for the war. In answer, over 30,000 men offered their services. This response earned for Tennessee the nickname "Volunteer State."

Among the Tennesseans to serve in the Mexican War were Gideon J. Pillow, Benjamin F. Cheatham, George W. Maney, and William B. Bate, all later to become generals in the Confederate army. From outside of Tennessee fought other men such as Jefferson Davis and Robert E. Lee, whose names would become immortal.

The end of the Mexican War in 1847 initiated well over a decade of relative peace and prosperity for the United States. The peace that America enjoyed outside of her borders, however, was marred by internal struggles. The southern states had remained predominantly agricultural, while the Industrial Revolution had begun to change the North into a nation of factory workers and merchants. The economic interests of the two sections grew more antagonistic as the years passed, and their representatives in Congress engaged in increasingly bitter debates over such issues as internal improvements, tariffs, and slavery.

Flag of the United States from 1859 to 1861

The sectional differences climaxed in the presidential election of 1860. Four men ran for president that year. The winner, Republican Abraham Lincoln, was the candidate of a party pledged to support the interests of the North and did not appear on the ballot or campaign in the southern states. He received less than forty percent of the popular vote, with less than two million votes cast for him, and almost three million against. Because the opposition was split three ways, however, Lincoln was elected.

Less than one month after Lincoln was officially declared the winner, a convention of the people of South Carolina declared the union dissolved, and South Carolina was once again an independent state. Six months later the people of Tennessee would volunteer to remove their star from the "Stars and Stripes" and place it upon the banner of a new southern nation.

CHAPTER 11
The Confederate States of America

After Lincoln's election many people of the South felt that they would no longer be able to enjoy the "domestic tranquility" or enjoy "the blessings of liberty" promised by the Constitution. The people of South Carolina elected delegates to a state convention in December 1860, and on December 20 the convention adopted an ordinance repealing the ordinance adopted by an earlier convention in 1788 ratifying the Constitution of the United States, and declaring that

> the union . . . between South Carolina and other States, under the name of the 'United States of America,' is hereby dissolved.

She was joined in January by Mississippi, Florida, Alabama, Georgia, and Louisiana, and on February 4, 1861 delegates from those six states met in a convention in Montgomery, Alabama to form a new federal government known as the Confederate States of America.

Other southern states called conventions as well, but of these only Texas was soon to join the new nation. Her lone star became a part of the Confederate constellation on March 2, 1861, the twenty-fifth anniversary of Texan independence from Mexico. The rest of the South decided to take a wait-and-see attitude towards Lincoln's government, and were willing to give him a chance to govern the union fairly.

Among the more patient southern states was Tennessee. Many Tennesseans sympathized with their more southern neighbors and believed in the cause of southern independence. Among these were Governor Isham G. Harris and a large number of the members of the legislature. Governor Harris called an extra session of the General Assembly on January 7, 1861, and the legislature passed a resolution calling for an election for a convention to discuss secession. The election was held on February 9, 1861, and the call for a convention was defeated. While the vote against the convention had a majority of only about 53 percent, the vote for pro-Union delegates to the convention had a majority of almost four to one. Tennessee was firmly in the union, for the time being.

In the meantime, the Confederate States continued to develop their new government and to seek a peaceful national existence. A constitution almost identical to that of the United States was adopted, ambassadors were sent to the United States, as well as to the governments of Europe, to negotiate treaties of peace and friendship, and a flag was adopted. The flag of the new nation was first raised on March 4, 1861, the same day that Lincoln was inaugurated President of the United States. The Confederate flag was similar to the flag of the United States, with a white star on the blue background to represent each state of the Confederacy, but with the thirteen stripes replaced by three bars. This modification of the "Stars and Stripes" was known as the "Stars and Bars."

During the first month of his presidency, Lincoln's administration held indirect negotiations with the Confederate peace commissioners in Washington. Of major concern were the federal garrisons which occupied Fort Sumter at Charleston, South Carolina, and Fort Pickens at Pensacola, Florida. Lincoln, through Secretary of State Seward, allowed the Confederates to believe that he intended to allow Fort Sumter's garrison to evacuate, but only after supplies had run out so that it could not be said he had unnecessarily backed down. In reality, however, an expedition was being prepared to resupply and reinforce the fort.

On April 12, 1861, with the Union reinforcement fleet outside Charleston harbor, Confederate General Beauregard demanded the surrender of the fort. The demand was refused and the opening shots of the war were fired. Three days later Lincoln issued a call for 75,000 men to form an army for the invasion and conquest of the Confederate States.

Lincoln's call for troops asked for Tennessee to send two regiments. Governor Harris replied by telegraph on the seventeenth, saying, "Tennessee will not furnish a single man for purposes of coercion but 50,000 if necessary for the defence of our rights and those of our southern brothers." While the election of an abolitionist president by a party dedicated only to the interests of one section of the union was not enough to drive Tennessee from the union, a war against free states for purposes of conquest would do so. On April 25, 1861, Governor Harris called the legislature back into session, and on May 6 the General Assembly passed a bill calling for an election to ratify a Declaration of Independence. On the eighth day of June the people voted for secession by a majority of 70 percent, and on the second of July Tennessee was admitted to the Confederate States of America as the eleventh state.

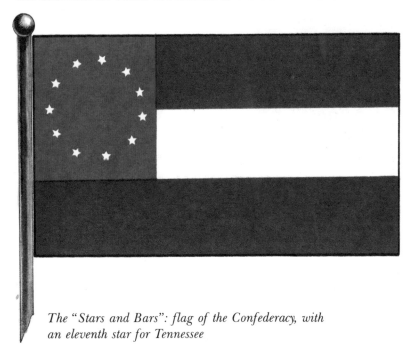

The "Stars and Bars": flag of the Confederacy, with an eleventh star for Tennessee

On Monday, the seventeenth of June, 1861, members of the General Assembly once again came to Nashville to prepare for the first regular session of the legislature to convene after the election approving secession. That evening a ceremony was held at the capitol in which, for the first time, the flag of the Confederate States of America with a new eleventh star for Tennessee was raised over the state capitol.

The "Stars and Bars" would continue to fly over the Confederate States for almost two more years, with the number of stars growing to thirteen after the admission of Missouri on November 28 and of Kentucky on December 10, 1861. War soon proved the flag to be inadequate, however, for it too closely resembled the flag of the enemy. By the end of 1861 the armies were replacing the national flag in the field with battle flags more easily distinguished from the "Stars and Stripes."

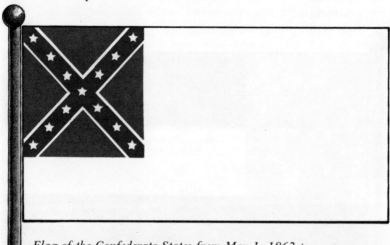

Flag of the Confederate States from May 1, 1863 to March 4, 1865

Flag of the Confederate States since March 4, 1865

The Confederate States of America

On the first day of May, 1861, the Confederate States Congress adopted a new flag for the Southern nation. The second national flag of the Confederacy was entirely different from the flag of the old union. The blue canton with stars was replaced by the blue-crossed red battle flag of the Army of Northern Virginia, while the red and white bars gave way to a field of pure white. The "Stainless Banner" served as the Confederate flag for almost two years. Some officers of the navy, however, felt that its white field was a problem. At a distance it was not very visible, and when hanging limp some perceived that it could be mistaken for a flag of truce. As a result, in the waning days of the war, the Confederate Congress modified the Confederate flag by changing its proportions and adding a broad red bar to the fly edge. This would be the last flag to fly over an independent South.

CHAPTER 12
Confederate Battle Flags

The Confederate States chose the "Stars and Bars" as their flag because of a strong sentimental attachment felt for the old flag by the people of the South. The Battle of Manassas in July 1861, however, showed the error of adopting a flag so similar to that of the enemy. In the smoke and haze of battle it was often difficult to distinguish stripes from bars, and on several occasions mistakes were made because of the inability to recognize a flag.

After the battle, General Beauregard spoke about the flag problem with Congressman William Porcher Miles of South Carolina, who was chairman of the Congressional Committee on Flag and Seal. He told Beauregard that Congress would not change the flag. As an alternative, Miles showed the general a flag which he had designed, and which Congress had rejected, suggesting that it might be used as a regimental battle flag in place of the Confederate flag. Beauregard and General Joseph E. Johnston took Miles's design, and had a version of it made and issued to the Confederate Army in Virginia in late 1861. This would become the famous Confederate Battle Flag.

Several Tennessee regiments fought under these flags on the battlefields of Virginia, Maryland, and Pennsylvania. Those Tennesseans would fight and die for Southern independence at such places as Sharpsburg, Chancellorsville, Gettysburg, and Petersburg.

Most Tennessee troops, however, fought closer to their homes, often on their own soil, in the western theatre's Army of Tennessee. The generals of that army also adopted battle flags for their regiments, but these were not uniform throughout the army as was the case in Virginia.

When the western army was organized at Corinth, Mississippi in the spring of 1862 by General Beauregard, it was given the name "Army of the Mississippi." The First Corps of that army was commanded by Lieutenant General Leonidas Polk, who was also bishop of the Episcopal Diocese of Louisiana. Polk's flag was an upright

Battle flag of a Tennessee regiment of the Army of Northern Virginia

Battle flag of a Tennessee regiment of General Polk's corps

red cross with white stars on a field of blue. Most of the Tennessee troops in the army were assigned to this corps.

In April 1862 there were three Tennessee infantry regiments in the Second Corps of the army under the command of General Braxton Bragg. The battle flags issued to those troops were ordered by General Beauregard, and were similar in design to the flags issued in Virginia.

The Third Corps of the Army of the Mississippi was commanded by General William J. Hardee, and included six regiments of Tennessee infantry. General Hardee had designed for his troops a white-bordered blue battle flag with a white disc in the center. His regiments would often paint their unit designations on the white disc.

Under these flags, as well as the Confederate "Stars and Bars," Tennessee soldiers would fight for their state's independence on the Tennessee fields of Shiloh and Murfreesboro. These flags also guided Tennesseans in battles outside of their state at such places as

Battle flag of a Tennessee regiment of
General Bragg's corps

Battle flag of a Tennessee regiment of General Hardee's corps

Perryville, Kentucky and Chickamauga in Georgia. Before the Battle of Murfreesboro (Stone's River) began in December 1862, the army was renamed the "Army of Tennessee."

By the time the army went into winter quarters around Dalton, Georgia in December 1863 many of these flags were worn and torn beyond recognition. The new army commander, General Joseph E. Johnston, ordered new standard battle flags issued to his regiments as the winter came to an end. Those flags were issued to all regiments except those of General Cleburne's division. Cleburne's regiments insisted that they be allowed to continue fighting under the blue flag designed by General Hardee.

Among the most famous of Tennessee's military leaders was the great cavalry commander, Lieutenant General Nathan Bedford Forrest. About half of the approximately thirty regiments composing his cavalry corps in 1864 and 1865 were Tennesseans. Forrest's Cavalry Corps was issued battle flags manufactured for the quartermaster of the Department of Alabama, Mississippi, and East Louisiana. These flags were similar to those issued to the Army of Tennessee at Dalton, Georgia, but had only twelve stars.

Battle flag of a Tennessee regiment of the Army of Tennessee, 1864–1865

Battle flag of a Tennessee regiment of General Forrest's cavalry

CHAPTER 13
Return to the "Stars and Stripes"

On May 9, 1865, one month after Lee's surrender at Appomattox, General Forrest surrendered his cavalry corps to the forces of the United States. The Tennesseans under his command were the last men of the Volunteer State to bear arms under the flag of the Confederate States.

In his farewell address General Forrest made the observation that, while civil war "naturally engenders feelings of animosity, hatred, and revenge," it was the duty of the Confederates "to divest ourselves of all such feelings." He told his men:

> You *have been* good soldiers; you *can be* good citizens. Obey the laws, preserve your honor, and the Government to which you have surrendered can afford to be, and will be magnanimous.

Flag of the United States from 1865 to 1867

And so the impoverished soldiers of Tennessee returned to what was left of their homes and families.

The "reconstructed" government of Tennessee, however, would prove far from magnanimous. The reconstruction governor was William G. Brownlow, a Methodist minister and editor of *Brownlow's Knoxville Whig*. He was a bitter and vindictive man who harbored strong prejudices against Catholics, Irishmen, Presbyterians, Baptists, Democrats, and anyone having any connection in the slightest way with the Confederacy. Because of his outspoken opposition to the Confederacy, he became the leader of Tennessee's "Tories," and was elected governor by them in 1865. Brownlow was the only candidate whose name was allowed on the ballot.

Brownlow's regime was marked by a spirit of vengeance. Every Tennessean who had, directly or indirectly, in any way aided the Confederacy was stripped of the right to vote or in any way participate in state government. He assumed dictatorial powers, and saw

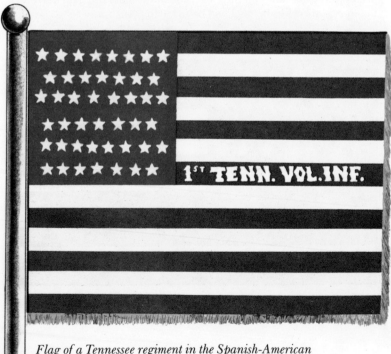

Flag of a Tennessee regiment in the Spanish-American War

that his will was enforced by military control and supervision of elections, when elections were allowed.

In 1867 Brownlow was reelected governor after a campaign marked by such arbitrary use of power that his opponent finally ceased to campaign. After the election, Brownlow had his legislature elect him to the United States Senate, to a seat which would not become vacant until 1869. But this time his quest for power proved a blessing in disguise. In 1869 Brownlow began an undistinguished term in the U.S. Senate, and the moderate Speaker of the Senate of the state of Tennessee, DeWitt Clinton Senter, became governor.

Governor Senter used the gubernatorial powers usurped by Brownlow to restore the vote to all male citizens of the state. In 1870 Tennessee once again had a freely elected government, and the state began the long road to true reconstruction.

The separation of the Southern states from the union had resulted in war, and the ferocity of that war and its aftermath kept the South from returning to full participation in the family of American states for many years afterwards. As the nineteenth century approached its end, another war would help to heal the old wounds.

In 1898 war erupted between the United States and Spain. The "Volunteer State" once again responded, offering her full quota of men and more. From that time to the present, whenever Liberty called for help, she could count on the volunteer spirit of Tennessee to answer her, and answer loudly.

PART III

FLAGS OF TENNESSEE'S CITIES AND COUNTIES

FLAGS OF TENNESSEE

Tennesseans have always believed that government functions best when it is close to the people. As a result, the state is divided into ninety-five counties, which contain almost one thousand cities and towns. Because Tennessee has so many local governments, the researcher has a great chore just to determine whether those governments have flags. Illustrating and describing the symbols of all of those governments could itself comprise a large publication.

Therefore, these chapters will discuss the flags of only a few of Tennessee's communities. The flags illustrated here, however, represent the local governments of about half of the population of the state.

CHAPTER 14
County Flags

CARTER COUNTY

One of the older counties, Carter was created in 1796, the same year Tennessee became a state. It was carved out of Washington County, and comprised the area which the failed state of Franklin had set up as Wayne County. The county was named in honor of Landon Carter, first Speaker of the Senate of the state of Franklin, and later that state's Secretary of State. Part of Carter County's territory was cut off to create Johnson County in 1836.

The flag of Carter County

The flag of Carter County is a red field bordered on its upper and lower edges by blue stripes. Centered on the field is a gold-edged seal which recalls "The Lost State of Franklin" and the date of the establishment of the county, "1796." The center of the seal features representations of a covered bridge and Fort Watauga, with a tribute to "The Wataugans," who, in 1772, established the first government in what was to become Tennessee. Because the people there were so far from any established government, they created the Watauga Association, governed by what is reputed to have been the first written constitution west of the Appalachians.

The flag of Carter County was designed by Todd Pate, a seventh-grade student at Happy Valley Middle School, and was adopted by the county legislative body on October 15, 1984.

DAVIDSON COUNTY

In 1783 the state of North Carolina established Davidson County in what were then its extreme western territories, now Middle Tennessee. The county was named in honor of Brigadier General William Lee Davidson, a distinguished North Carolina officer in the revolutionary army. The county seat was established at Nashville.

In 1963 the government of Davidson County consolidated with the city of Nashville to create a metropolitan government for both the city and the county. In December of that year a new flag was created for the people of Davidson County.

Flag of the metropolitan government of Nashville and Davidson County

The flag of the metropolitan government is patterned after the state flag, with the colors and central device changed. The crimson field of the Tennessee flag was changed to blue for Davidson County, and the blue stripe on the fly edge became deep gold. The resolution adopting the flag states that the blue stands for the courage and conviction of the county's leaders throughout history, while the gold denotes the richness of its land and resources.

The round blue field and three stars of the state flag were replaced by the seal of the Metropolitan Government of Nashville and Davidson County, set within the points of a compass. The seal combines the eagle and shield of the old county seal with the Indian of the former seal of the city of Nashville. The Indian, said to represent the Cherokee chief Oconostota, is holding a skull and war spear, which he and James Robertson buried between them as a sign of peace shortly after the founding of Nashville.

HAMILTON COUNTY

Hamilton County was created in 1819 and was named for Alexander Hamilton. Later, the territory of the county was increased with a portion of the lands acquired from the Cherokee Nation in the events leading up to the infamous Trail of Tears.

Flag of Hamilton County

The flag of Hamilton County was adopted by the county council on December 17, 1963, and the first flag of that pattern was presented to the council on May 6, 1964. The flag was designed by James Christian, a student at Chattanooga High School.

Hamilton County's flag features a blue silhouette map of the county on a white field. Above the map is an arched red ribbon with the name "HAMILTON COUNTY" in white letters, while a straight ribbon in the same color spells out "TENNESSEE" below. Centered on the map is a white seal with representations in blue of a log cabin and an industrial plant, and displaying the word "TRADITION" above and the word "INDUSTRY" below in blue letters. Councilman Jack D. Mayfield, who originated the idea of adopting a county flag, described it as a banner "recognizing past accomplishments of our citizens and expressing an awareness of our citizenship responsibilities."

HARDIN COUNTY

Hardin County lies in West Tennessee. It is bisected by the Tennessee River and is bordered on the south by Alabama and Mississippi. Hardin County was established in 1819 out of part of the lands purchased from the Chickasaw Nation the previous year. The county was named for Colonel Joseph Hardin, a revolutionary war veteran and Speaker of the Assembly of the state of Franklin.

Flag of Hardin County

Hardin County's flag is a blue field with a gold-bordered seal in the center. The gold border of the seal is inscribed with the county name. The center displays a map of the county in grey on a sky blue background. Above the map is a gold ribbon with the name "Joseph Hardin" in old English letters, and a representation of the tri-star disc of the Tennessee flag in blue and grey. The date "1819" is below the map on the seal, and the map is flanked by an iris bloom and a mockingbird, both symbols of Tennessee. The map itself identifies the cities and towns of the county, and such important historical sites as the Shiloh battlefield.

KNOX COUNTY

Knox County was established by the legislature of the Territory of the United States South of the River Ohio in 1792, and its county seat, Knoxville, became the territorial capital that same year. The county was named for Major General Henry Knox, Washington's chief of artillery during the Revolution and secretary of war in President Washington's cabinet.

Flag of Knox County

The Knox County Commission adopted a flag on March 6, 1979. Like the flag of metropolitan Davidson County, Knox County's flag is inspired by the design of the Tennessee flag. The field is blue and the fly end is edged with a narrow white stripe and a broader red stripe. In the center is the county seal in black on a white background, separated from the blue field by a broad red border. The design of the county seal is copied from the Great Seal of the state of Tennessee.

MAURY COUNTY

Maury County in Middle Tennessee was named for Abram Maury, a surveyor and state senator from Williamson County. Maury County was carved out of Williamson County in 1807.

Flag of Maury County

Maury County's flag is a blue field with a central seal surrounded by a green laurel leaf. Above it is a single grey star. The buff-colored seal has a grey border inscribed with the county name and a grey circle in the center displaying the date of the county's founding, 1807. Arrayed around the date on the buff field are an acorn, a representation of a factory, and a mule's head. Maury County has historically been a center of mule breeding, and an important festival in the county is the annual Mule Day parade held in Columbia.

SHELBY COUNTY

Shelby County is in the extreme southwest corner of the state, and includes the city of Memphis. The county was established in 1819 out of a portion of the land acquired in the Chickasaw Purchase of 1818. The county was named for Isaac Shelby, a revolutionary war hero and governor of Kentucky, who together with Andrew Jackson arranged the treaty by which West Tennessee was purchased from the Chickasaw Nation.

Flag of Shelby County

The flag of Shelby County was designed in 1970 by Mrs. Ellen Davies Rodgers, the county historian. The bright green field of the flag is decorated with the county seal in gold with black details. Like the seal of Knox County, the Shelby County seal takes its design from the Great Seal of the state.

SULLIVAN COUNTY

Sullivan County was established by the North Carolina legislature in 1779, and was the second county founded in what was to become Tennessee. The county was named for Major General John

Sullivan, a revolutionary war leader, member of the Continental Congress, and later governor of New Hampshire.

Flag of Sullivan County

The flag of Sullivan County was adopted by the Board of Commissioners on February 15, 1988. It was designed by David Gladson of Kingsport, an eighth-grade student at Lynn View Middle School.

The Sullivan County flag features a blue union and a field of three bars of red, white, and red, reminiscent of the original national flag of the Confederate States. The union, however, extends down the entire width of the flag, and is separated from the bars by a serrated edge. Centered on the union is a representation of the Great Seal of Sullivan County.

The flag is unusual in that it has additional devices added to the fly end. On each bar is a disc or circle, white on the red bars and red on the white one. Superimposed over the discs are, from top to bottom: a scroll, representing learning; the outline of a factory, representing industry; and an ear of corn, representing agriculture.

CHAPTER 15
City Flags

CHATTANOOGA

Chattanooga was established in 1839 and is the county seat of Hamilton County. There is apparently no record that the city government ever officially adopted Chattanooga's flag, but it has been used in the city for over two decades. The flag is almost identical to the state flag, Tennessee's three stars having been replaced by a single star surrounded by a wreath.

Flag of Chattanooga

CLARKSVILLE

Clarksville, which was founded in 1784, is the county seat of Montgomery County. The city flag was adopted on September 25, 1987, and was designed by Kay Darnell Drew. The flag's field is composed of three vertical bars of blue, white, and blue. The white bar is about twice the width of the blue bars. In the center of the flag is a seal with a red border inscribed with the city's name and founding date in gold.

Flag of Clarksville

The seal displays a shield surrounded by an oak wreath in gold outline and surmounted by three gold stars, for the Grand Divisions of the state. The star for Middle Tennessee, in which Clarksville is located, is larger than the other two. The shield is divided by blue and white wavy lines, representing the Cumberland and Red rivers. In the upper portion of the shield are symbols for justice and learning, while the lower section displays emblems of agriculture and industry.

GOODLETTSVILLE

Although not incorporated until 1958, Goodlettsville, in northern Davidson County, has been a thriving community for over 200 years, and is claimed by some to be the oldest settlement in Middle Tennessee.

The flag of Goodlettsville was designed by Mrs. Gertrude M. Stamper and was adopted by the Goodlettsville City Commission in 1975 as a project of the Goodlettsville Bicentennial Commission. The flag is divided horizontally into two colors, red over blue. In

Flag of Goodlettsville

the upper hoist corner is placed the blue circle and three stars of the Tennessee state flag. Centered on the flag is a circular field of white, on which are depicted a Tennessee cedar tree and a log cabin. The evergreen tree represents the freshness of youth, hope, and life. The log cabin is representative of the first home of Kasper Mansker, the city's original settler, whose first station and fort were built on the future site of Goodlettsville in 1779 or 1780.

JACKSON

Named for Andrew Jackson, the town of Jackson was first laid out in 1822, and became the county seat of Madison County, which had been founded the previous year. Jackson is located near the center of West Tennessee, and soon became something of a capital for the western district. The Supreme Court of Tennessee, along with the Court of Appeals and the Court of Criminal Appeals, hold their Western Division sessions in Jackson.

The flag of the city of Jackson features a red-bordered, white silhouette map of Tennessee on a sky blue field. A red dot marks

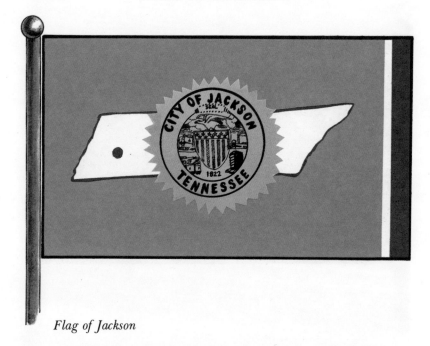

Flag of Jackson

the geographic location of Jackson in West Tennessee. Overlaying the central portion of the map is the seal of the city in black on gold. As is done with the flags of several other Tennessee counties and cities, the fly edge of Jackson's flag copies the Tennessee flag in having two stripes running the width of the flag: a red stripe separated from the blue field by one of white.

KNOXVILLE

Knoxville was founded in 1792 at the site of James White's fort on the Holston River in Knox County. Like the county, it was named for United States Secretary of War James Knox, and the city became the capital of the Southwest Territory. With statehood Knoxville became the state capital, and remained the seat of government for Tennessee until 1813, with one final session of the legislature being held there in 1817 before the capital was permanently moved to Middle Tennessee.

The flag of Knoxville was adopted on October 16, 1896, making it the oldest municipal flag in use in Tennessee. The field of the flag is white, with a light blue square equal in size to one-third the width of the flag in the upper hoist corner, and a red square of

Flag of Knoxville

similar size in the lower hoist corner. Running horizontally from the blue and red squares to the fly end of the flag are two bars of black, each one-half the width of the squares, and so positioned that a white bar of equal width separates them from the outer edges of the flag. Centered on the field of the flag, inside a winged wheel of gold, are the arms of the city of Knoxville over the date "1792."

MANCHESTER

Manchester was founded in 1836, the same year Coffee County was established. The city was chartered in 1838, and is the county seat.

The flag of Manchester was chosen in a competition held in May 1986. The winning entry was designed by Kevin Seals, a student at Central High School. The flag follows the theme of the Tennessee flag, with the red and blue colors reversed. In the red disc the three stars of Tennessee are replaced by a white silhouette map of the state, with a small blue star indicating the geographic location of Manchester. The white circle separating the red disc from the blue field displays the name "MANCHESTER" and the date "1836."

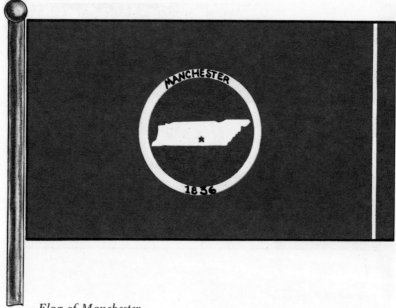

Flag of Manchester

MEMPHIS

Memphis was laid out on the Chickasaw Bluff overlooking the Mississippi River in 1819 by a party composed of Andrew Jackson, Isaac Shelby, and John Overton. It quickly became a thriving river port, and within forty years was the most important commercial center in West Tennessee. Although the city was virtually depopulated by the yellow fever epidemics of the 1870s and 1880s, Memphis rebounded in the early twentieth century, and is now the largest city in Tennessee.

The law authorizing the flag of Memphis is found in section 1–7 of the City Code of 1967. The field of the flag is composed of white, red, and blue, with the white portion running the width of the flag at the hoist, and the red and blue portions in horizontal bars running from the white to the flag's fly edge. The line dividing the white portion from the red and blue portions runs at an angle that is roughly equal to the angle at which the Mississippi River runs along the boundary between West Tennessee and northern Mississippi on the east, and Arkansas on the west. The colored fields of the flag, therefore, represent the geographic location of

Flag of Memphis

Memphis at the juncture of those three states, with the red representing Tennessee, the blue Mississippi, and the white Arkansas.

Centered at the point where the three colors join is the seal of the city of Memphis in gold. The shape of the seal itself is unusual, being a square with rounded corners. Although the Memphis flag ordinance specifies that the lettering, illustrations, and inscription on the gold seal shall be in white, in practice the flags are made with those details in black, which is more heraldically correct and enhances visibility.

NASHVILLE

Nashville was established by a party led by James Robertson, which built its settlement, originally known as Nashborough, on the bluffs by French Lick that overlook the Cumberland River. The town took its name from Colonel Francis Nash, a revolutionary war hero from North Carolina. The town grew and thrived, and in 1843 became the permanent capital of Tennessee.

The flag of Nashville was inspired by the battle flag of the Confederate Army of Tennessee. The red field was crossed with a

Flag of Nashville

white saltire, and bordered on its outer edges in blue. At the junction of the cross was a single blue star. Around the star was a laurel wreath in gold, which terminated above in the letter "N."

With the consolidation of the city and county governments in 1962, the flag of the city of Nashville was replaced by the flag of the Metropolitan Government of Nashville and Davidson County.

PARIS

Named for the capital of France, the city of Paris, in Henry County, West Tennessee, was founded in 1823. Among its founding families were the Dunlaps (ancestors of the author) and the Porters (ancestors of the author's wife).

The flag of Paris is a tricolor of blue, white, and red, and is modeled after the flag of France. On the white panel of the flag is the seal of the city, in blue. This flag was adopted by the city commission on April 1, 1982.

Flag of Paris

An Essay on the Designing of Flags

On March 4, 1861, the Committee on Flag and Seal made a report to the Provisional Congress of the Confederate States of America on its activities in selecting a design for the flag of the new nation. In its report, the committee observed that

> A flag should be simple, readily made, and, above all, capable of being made up in bunting. It should be different from the flag of any other country, place, or people. It should be readily distinguishable at a distance. The colors should be well contrasted and durable, and, lastly, and not the least important, it should be effective and handsome.

Simple, distinctive, handsome: these are the adjectives that should govern anyone who sets out to design a flag. Intricate designs should be avoided. Words should almost never be placed on a flag. Colors touching one another should contrast well. Most countries adhere to these standards in their flags. Over sixty-two percent of the member countries of the United Nations have flags with simple features employing three colors or less. Only about ten percent have features which are so complicated that a citizen would have difficulty making his or her own country's flag.

Despite this simplicity of design, very few countries have identical flags. Little Monaco on the European side of the Mediterranean Sea shares a flag of red over white with Indonesia on the other side of the world. Since the Christmas Revolution in 1989 tore the badge of communism from its flag, Romania has joined Chad and Andorra in flying a blue, yellow, and red tricolor. These instances, however, are the exceptions that prove the rule.

Besides black and white, the most commonly used colors are red, blue, green, and yellow. Bophuthatswana, India, Ireland, Ivory Coast, Niger, South Africa, and Zambia use orange in their flags, while Transkei is alone in the use of brown in its tricolor.

When one leaves the realm of national or federal flags, the observance of the rule of simplicity and distinctiveness is not as apparent. The flags of the American states are good examples, in many cases, of how not to design a flag. Some states, such as Alaska and Texas, have simple, distinctive, and handsome flags. Thirty-seven of the states, however, have more or less complex designs that employ the use of words or mottoes. Twenty states have merely placed the state seal or coat of arms on a blue field, and ten states have done so on a field other than blue.

Vexillography—the art of designing flags—is an offshoot of the ancient art of heraldry. In heraldic terms, "colors" include red, blue, and green, while white and yellow were termed "metals" to represent silver and gold. One of the earliest rules one learns in the study of heraldry is that color should not be placed on color, nor metal on metal. The practical reason for this is to provide for clarity and distinctiveness in a design.

Imagine a flag having a blue cross on a red field. While blue and red are certainly distinguishable colors, each is more sharply defined and distinctive if the blue cross is separated from the red field by a narrow white or yellow border. Likewise, if one pictures a flag composed of a yellow cross on a white field, it is clear that even at a short distance the cross will be hard to see, but if edged in a color, both the white and the yellow will be complemented.

When designing a flag, the theme should be kept simple. Many nations and movements use simple tricolor designs, either vertical, like the flag of France, or horizontal, as with the Lithuanian flag. In an effort to create more distinctive banners, geometric designs may be added to the tricolor field, such as the triangle found on the flags of the Bahamas and Sudan, or a perpendicular bar such as used on the flags of the Transvaal and the United Arab Emirates.

Many people wish to incorporate some distinctive emblem representative of their country or movement into their flag. These too should be kept as simple as possible. Good examples of simplicity are the Canadian maple leaf and Israel's star of David.

Certain terminology is used to describe various parts and design elements of flags. The accompanying glossary will help with some of this vocabulary.

Simple, distinctive, handsome: these words should be the hallmark of a flag. A flag is a statement, an artistic expression of a people or an idea. Like a good advertising trademark or political slogan, a well designed flag should be identifiable at a glance.

Glossary

CANTON: The upper left-hand corner of a flag. This is sometimes referred to as the "union" of the flag.

FLY: The length of a flag.

FLY EDGE: The width of the flag at the point farthest from the staff.

HOIST: The width of the flag at the point nearest the staff.

IMPALED: A design device in which the field of a flag or coat of arms is divided in half vertically, with different designs appearing in each half of the field.

QUARTERED: A design device in which the field of a flag or coat of arms is divided into four panels, two above and two below, with two to four different designs appearing in the four panels.

SALTIRE: A cross on a flag or coat of arms in an "x" form. Also called a Saint Andrew's cross.

VEXILLOGRAPHY: The art of designing flags.

VEXILLOLOGY: The study of flags.